Walking with God or the Devil, Which? *and* The King's Gold Mine

by

Rev. Bud Robinson

First Fruits Press
Wilmore, Kentucky
2015

Walking with God or the Devil, Which? and *The King's Gold Mine* by
Bud Robinson

Published by First Fruits Press, ©2015
Previously Published by the Pentecostal Publishing Company, c1900

ISBN: 9781621711704 (print), 9781621711698 (digital)

Digital version at
http://place.asburyseminary.edu/firstfruitsheritagematerial/88/

Robinson, Bud, 1860-1942.
     Walking with God or the Devil, which? : and The King's gold
     mine / by Bud Robinson
     29 pages ; 21 cm.
     Wilmore, Ky. : First Fruits Press, ©2015
     Reprint. Previously published: Louisville, Ky. : Pentecostal
     Publishing Company, c1900.
     ISBN: 9781621711704 (pbk.)
     1. Bible. -- O.T. -- Genesis III, 8 -- Sermons. 2. Bible. -- N.T. --
     Corinthians, 2nd, VI-VII, 3 -- Sermons. 3. Sermons, American 4.
     Methodist Church – Sermons. I. Title. II. The King's gold mine.
     BS1235 .R62 2015

                                                                    248

Cover design by Amelia Hegle

First Fruits Press
The Academic Open Press of Asbury Theological Seminary
204 N. Lexington Ave., Wilmore, KY 40390
859-858-2236
first.fruits@asburyseminary.edu
asbury.to/firstfruits

Walking With God

Or The

Devil, ... Which?

And

The King's Gold Mine

By

Rev. Bud Robinson

Pentecostal Publishing Company
Louisville Kentucky

WALKING WITH GOD OR THE DEVIL ... WHICH?

In Genesis 3:8 we read, "And they heard the voice of the Lord walking in the garden in the cool of the day," and in the book of Job, first chapter and seventh verse, "And the Lord said unto Satan, Whence comest thou? Then Satan answered the Lord, and said, From going to and fro in the earth, and from walking up and down in it."

My friends, we have before us two of the greatest generals that ever crossed swords on earth. One rules heaven and the other hell, and the country that you and I live in is in dispute, and we find these commanders walking up and down on this earth seeking companionship. They are both seekers—they are beating their drums and calling for volunteers, and you have to walk with one or the other of these generals. You see you are a free agent, and this war is in the country where you live, and you are compelled to take sides with one or the other, and then you are so constructed that you can't go through this country without a companion. You see we are of a very puny make-up. There is a place in your heart that must be full all the time, and if you are not walking with God and filled with Him, then you are walking with the Devil and you are filled with him.

You see, in some respects God and the Devil are just alike. They are both walking up and down the earth—they are both seeking you. God wants you to glorify Him, and, of course, the Devil wants you to glorify him. They are both looking at you, and if God don't get you, the Devil will. They both take everybody they can get. We read in 2 Chron. 16:9, "For the eyes of the Lord run to and fro throughout the whole earth to show himself strong in behalf of them whose heart is perfect toward him." So you see, my friend, God is looking for somebody to walk with Him, and there is nothing that pleases God better than to find a fellow that will walk with Him. In Psalm 84:11, He said, "No good thing will He withhold from them that walk uprightly." Well, glory to God, heaven is plunder to the man that is walking with God, and God has nothing too good for the man that will link arms with Him and walk through this country by His side. With all God's greatness and riches and glory in heaven, He seems to have left it all, and He is down here walking up and down in the earth looking for some fellow to walk with Him. It seems like God would rather walk with a man on earth than to sit on a throne and rule a universe; and it matters not how poor and sinful and wretched the fellow is, if he is tired of sin and evil and immorality, and sick of himself and disgusted with the Devil, there is nothing that would please God better than to link arms with that poor sinner and pull him out of his poverty, and put shoes on his feet and a ring on his hand, and clothe him with the robes of righteousness, and order the fatted calf killed.

Well, thank God, He has been able to find a few followers that were willing to walk with Him, and He has left nothing undone to prove to this old world that He was making the fellow happy that was walking with Him. So you see, my friend, God is doing all that a God of love and mercy can do to make you one of the purest, holiest, happiest and best men on earth. And the Devil is doing all a mighty Devil can do to make you one of the most corrupt, vile, degraded, sin-cursed, devil-ridden, hell-bound men that walks on earth. The Devil is a mighty general; his black flag is floating over multiplied thousands of Adam's fallen race, and he is robbing heaven and populating hell with human souls. My friend, if he can persuade you to walk with him he will put hell in you while you are on earth, and then put you in hell after you die. The only use the Devil has for you, is for you to commit sin for him; and when you do it, you dishonor God, degrade the human family, glorify the Devil, and become a co-worker with him. My friend, if you will stop for a few hours and just walk through the Devil's camp and see the awful wreckage of his soldiers, and hear their groans and shrieks and wails as they die in darkness and despair, you will be convinced that the Devil is the greatest enemy his followers ever had.

Come, friend, and walk with me through the camp of the Lord, and let us see if we can see any difference between the soldiers and the camps of these two commanders. The first one of the Lord's soldiers I want you to look at is Enoch. We read in Genesis 5:22, that Enoch walked with God three hundred years. So you see that God found a man going in the same direction that He was going, and it was so easy for them to walk together. After a stroll of three hundred years we find Enoch and the Lord enjoying each other's society so much, and their companionship so delightful, that the Lord proposed to Enoch to go home with Him and stay all night, and, of course, Enoch did not refuse. And he went up to the country where the Lord lives, and he met so many of the old soldiers there, and they had such a shine on their faces, and they had so many things to tell him about the city that he seemed to forget all about this country—and then, to his surprise, the sun has never set there, and he has been there in that city with the Lord and the old soldiers five thousand years, shining and shouting, and to his great satisfaction there has never been one night there, and of course, Enoch could not very well come back to this country until he had stayed one night with the Lord. You see, friend, a day in the Lord's country is as everlasting as God Himself, for the Lord God is the light thereof.

Now, friend, as we have been watching the Lord and one of His soldiers for awhile, let us turn our eyes and just look at one of the Devil's soldiers for a few minutes. We see a young man by the name of Cain joining the Devil's army. The first thing the Devil puts him at is disbelieving God. The next work he has for him to do is to murder his brother, and as the earth opens her mouth to swallow the blood of his brother, we see Cain fleeing from home and crying out, "My punishment is greater than I can bear," and there was a mark put on him so that everybody that saw him would know that he was a murderer, and he was cursed from the face of the earth, and in sorrow and disgrace he walked up and down in the earth, a fugitive and a vagabond. My friend, will you stop long enough to hear Cain tell his experience that will throw a world of light on the subject. In Gen. 4:13, 14, "And Cain said unto the Lord, My punishment is greater than I can bear; behold, thou hast driven me out this day from the face of the earth, and from Thy face shall I be hid, and I shall be a fugitive and a vagabond in the earth, and it shall come to pass that every one that findeth me shall slay me." Now, reader, did you ever hear a testimony with more sorrow and sadness in it than this one? It looks like if the Devil had a heart that the testimony of Cain would break it.

Reader, just think of the difference between Enoch and Cain. Look at Enoch as he steps into a chariot and goes sweeping through the gates of the New Jerusalem, leaning on the everlasting arms. Now turn and look out there at Cain as he looks up from his poverty and misery and woe. You see the black-winged demons hovering over him, and you hear his awful wail, "My punishment is greater than I can bear."

Let us look at another of the Lord's soldiers for a few minutes. In Genesis 6:9, we read, These are the generations of Noah; Noah was a just man and perfect in his generation, and Noah walked with God." So you see, reader, here is another fellow that was willing to walk with God, and now let us see what the Lord did for him. We read in the eleventh chapter of Hebrews and seventh verse, "By faith Noah being warned of God of things not seen as yet, moved with fear, prepared an ark to the saving of his house; by which he condemned the world and became heir of the righteousness which is by faith." So you see, reader, God gave this man Noah the honor of building the only ark that was ever built, and when the creek got up higher than it had ever been before, Noah had the blessed privilege of moving into the ark with all his house, and he and all his floated over a river five miles deep and more than twelve months wide. Well, thank God for such deliverance as God brings to them that walk with Him.

Now look at another soldier from the Devil's camp. You remember a young man by the name of Saul. He started out in God's army and God blessed him above his fellows, and he had the finest prospects before him of any man in his land. God gave him great riches and honor, and it seemed God just piled good things around him, and he had everything that heart could wish, but finally the Devil succeeded in getting him to forsake God and join him. The Devil put him to doing his work, and of all the dark pictures you ever looked at you find them in the life of this young man. His friends left him, his fortune seemed to take the wings of the morning and flee away. He lost his national standing —his people forsook him—friends and fortune gone, and broken in health and his soul and body filled with evil spirits, we find him wandering about in darkness and wretchedness without a ray of hope, and finally you see him walking up and down in the earth, and crossing the hills and mountains on a dark, drizzly night seeking for a witch to call upon dead man, to see if he could get one ray of light to comfort his poor, broken, and sad heart. But all the witch tells him only increases his awful agony of soul, and he wanders about the rest of the night, and daybreak finds him in such awful sorrow and wretchedness that to end his miserable existence he feels would be a great relief, and you see him falling on his own sword, plunging it to his heart. You hear his awful wail as he dies without God.

Now, reader, just glance at this dying soldier as he lay there with his sword stuck through his body, and the Devil with all his imps shouting for joy, and just think of what this man was at one time, walking with God, fighting under the banner of righteousness, with the smiles of God on him and the fat of the land in his possession. Now see gloated-faced devils spreading out their black wings over him as he dies by his own hand. What an awful step that man took when he stepped down and out of God's company and linked arms with the Devil.

Now, reader, turn with me and let us look at one more soldier. In Genesis 17:1-3, we read, "And when Abram was ninety years old and nine, the Lord appeared to Abram and said unto him, I am the Almighty God; walk before me, and be thou perfect." So you see this man was to walk with God in perfection, and for one hundred and seventy-five years we see God and Abraham walking hand in hand. God had so much respect for Abraham He would not do anything in the country without sending angels to consult him. And God made an everlasting covenant with him and gave him all the land of Canaan for a possession, and God allowed the angels to come down from heaven and rest in Abraham's tent and stay with him till after dinner.

But few men in this world have had the honor of getting dinner for the angels, but Abraham had that honor because he was walking with God. And we read in the Bible that Abraham was the friend of God. Friend, did you know that that was never said of any other man on earth? And He is called the Father of the faithful in the Bible, another remarkable statement not said of any other man.

Well, glory to God, the man in all ages of the world that has walked with God has come out ahead. Well, *glory!*

THE KING'S GOLD MINE

or

The Conversion and Sanctification of the Disciples

You will find the Scripture lesson in the sixth chapter of 2 Corinthians and the first three verses of the seventh chapter.

CHAPTER VI

We then as workers together with him, beseech you also that ye receive not the grace of God in vain.

2. (For he saith, I have heard thee in a time accepted, and in the day of salvation have I succoured thee; behold, now is the accepted time; behold, now is the day of salvation.)

3. Giving no offence in anything, that the ministry be not blamed;

4. But in all things approving ourselves as the ministers of God, in much patience, in afflictions, in necessities, in distresses.

5. In stripes, in imprisonments, in tumults, in labors, in watchings, in fastings;

6. By pureness, by knowledge, by longsuffering, by kindness, by the Holy Ghost, by love unfeigned,

7. By the word of truth, by the power of God, by the armour of righteousness on the right hand and on the left.

8. By honor and dishonor, by evil report and good report: as deceivers, and yet true;

9. As unknown, and yet well known; as dying, and, behold, we live as chastened and not killed;

10. As sorrowful, yet always rejoicing; as poor, yet making many rich; as having nothing, and yet possessing all things.

11. O ye Corinthians, our mouth is open unto you, our heart is enlarged.

12. Ye are not straightened in us, but ye are straightened in your own bowels.

13. Now for a recompense in the same, (I speak as unto my children,) be ye also enlarged.

14. Be ye not unequally yoked together with unbelievers: for what fellowship hath the righteous with unrighteousness? and what communion hath light with darkness?

15. And what concord hath Christ with Belial? or what part hath he that believeth with an infidel?

16. And what agreement hath the temple of God with idols? for ye are the temple of the living God; as God hath said, I will dwell in them, and walk in them; and I will be their God, and they shall be my people.

17. Wherefore come out from among them, and be ye separate, saith the Lord, and touch not the unclean thing; and I will receive you.

18. And I will be a Father unto you, and ye shall be my sons and daughters, saith the Lord Almighty.

CHAPTER VII

Having therefore these promises, dearly beloved, let us cleanse ourselves from all filthiness of the flesh and spirit, perfecting holiness in the fear of God.

2. Receive us; we have wronged no man, we have corrupted no man, we have defrauded no man.

3. I speak not this to condemn you; for I have said before, that ye are in our hearts to die and live with you.

You will find the text in Luke 24:49. "And behold I send the promise of my Father upon you but tarry ye in the City of Jerusalem until ye be endued with power from on high." Now, if the disciples had never been converted, and were still in their sins at the time the Lord made this promise, then the promise of the Father and the enduement of power is nothing more or less than the new birth, but if they had been converted and were at that time the children of God, and not in a backslidden state, then the promise of the Father and the enduement of power is a blessing or a work of grace received by faith by the disciples subsequent to regeneration.

Now, if the disciples had not been converted before Pentecost, then we Second Blessing people are without a Scriptural warrant for our doctrine and we are preaching heresy and we are false teachers, and every church in the land ought to be branded as a set of heretics and fanatics and hobby riders, who ride a hobby without eyes or ears or legs, but listen to me, folks, just a minute. If the disciples had been converted before Pentecost and were not backslidden at Pentecost, then we Second Blessing people are Scriptural and orthodox, and the crowd that is preaching that the disciples were never converted until Pentecost are unscriptural and unorthodox, and are false teachers and the churches ought to be closed in their faces and every church in the land ought to be open to us.

Now, what say ye? I have stated the thing fair and Scriptural and reasonable, as every thinking man will admit, and now I affirm that the disciples were converted men before Pentecost and that they were not backslidden when they received the promise of the Father and the enduement of power. Now, the question naturally arises, can I prove it? and without any spirit of boasting but with a spirit of humility I say yes. I can prove it satisfactorily to every reasonable man on earth.

Now for the facts in the case. First, Jesus Christ laid down his own terms of discipleship. Well, now what were they? We will look at the old Book and let God's word answer. In Matt. 16:24 and Mark 8:34 and Luke 9:23 we have the terms of discipleship laid down by the Lord himself. Well, now what are they? Listen to him, He says, "Except ye deny yourself and take up your cross and follow me, ye cannot be my disciples." Now, my friend, Jesus Christ had a perfect right to make this test and thank God, it means as much today as it did nineteen hundred years ago.

The next question is, had the disciples left all and followed Jesus? Well, we will let the old Book answer again. See Matt. 19:27. Then answered Peter and said, Behold Master, we have forsaken all and followed Thee, what shall we have therefor," and Jesus answered in the 28th verse and said, "Verily I say unto you that ye which have followed me in the regeneration when the Son of man shall sit on the throne of his glory, ye also shall sit upon twelve thrones, judging the twelve tribes of Israel." I know Jesus Christ never gave any sinner the promise of sitting on a throne to judge the Israelites, and the fact that the disciples had forsaken all and followed Jesus, and had the promise from the Father of sitting on twelve thrones and judging the twelve tribes of Israel is at least one good Scriptural evidence that they were converted men.

We next notice that he had ordained these men before Pentecost and Jesus never ordained a sinner to preach the Gospel. See John 15:16, "Ye have not chosen me but I have chosen you and ordained you, that you should go forth and bring forth fruit, and that your fruit should remain, that whatsoever ye shall ask of the Father in my name, He may give it you." Now, any man with any reason will say that if these men had been chosen and ordained and sent out to gather fruit that they could not have been unregenerated sinners. Now, let's take a look at them as they went out to preach, some two or three years before Pentecost. In St. Mark's Gospel, 6:12, St. Mark says that they went out and preached that men should repent. That looks like strange doctrine to preach, that is for a sinner to preach; don't you think so? Well, at least it does to me. Now, the question to settle is, What is repentance? In Matt. 3:2, John the Baptist said, "Repent for the Kingdom of Heaven is at hand." John seems to think that repentance is something that a man has to do before he can get into the Kingdom or get the Kingdom into him, but while he commands us to repentance he does not tell us what repentance is. Again we see in Luke the 13th chapter and third verse, that Jesus Christ said, "Except ye repent ye shall all likewise perish." Here again we see the necessity of repentance but no explanation of what repentance is, but we turn to 2nd Cor., the 7th chapter and 9th and 10th verses, and St. Paul said that repentance is a Godly sorrow for sin that needeth not to be repented of, and while Mark said they preached repentance, St. Matthew said they preached the Kingdom of God. See Matt. 10:7. Jesus Christ said, "As ye go preach saying the Kingdom of Heaven is at hand;" here he tells them to preach the Kingdom, but he doesn't tell them what the Kingdom is in this text, but in St. Matt. 6th chapter and 33rd verse Jesus Christ said, "Seek ye first the Kingdom of God and His righteousness and all things shall be added unto you." He tells them to seek the Kingdom, but He doesn't tell them what it is. Again in Luke 17:21 Jesus Christ said, "For the kingdom of God is within you."

Here Jesus locates the Kingdom on the inside of the disciples. The reader will observe that in Matt. 10:7 Christ said, preach the Kingdom and in Matt. 6:33 He told them to seek the Kingdom, and now in Luke 17:21 He tells them that the Kingdom is within you, but nothing of the above text tells us just what it is, but thank the Lord, St. Paul tells us in the 14th chapter and 17th verse what the Kingdom of God is. He says in the 14th chapter and 17th verse that the Kingdom of God is not meat and drink but righteousness and peace and joy in the Holy Ghost. Now, if they were preaching repentance and the Kingdom of Heaven three years before Pentecost they were not preaching like a sinner would preach in the twentieth century. But we take another step. In St. Luke 9:6 Luke said they went through the towns preaching the Gospel. Now, the question is, what is the Gospel? Well, the good theologians tell us that the Gospel means good news, and I suppose it does, but we read in Rom. 1:6 where St. Paul said, I am not ashamed of the Gospel of Jesus Christ, for it, the gospel, is the power of God unto salvation to everyone that believeth. Now friend, hold your breath a moment and look at the above statement. Matthew said they preached the Kingdom; Mark said they preached repentance, and Luke said they preached the Gospel. Don't you think these young men the most zealous sinners you ever saw if they had not been converted, which the great bulk of the pulpits say they had not, but thank God, the holiness outfit says they had been converted, and we are proving it to you right now while you are reading these words, and you know it as well as you know you are alive.

We next notice that Christ sent out these men as preachers of the Gospel and not a set of unregenerated sinners. The reader will see in Matthew the 10th chapter, and in Mark 6th chapter, and Luke 9th chapter that they were sent out by our Lord, and in the 10th chapter of St. Luke, our dear Lord sent out seventy others to help carry on the work, and they came back rejoicing and saying, Lord, even the devils are subject to us through thy name, and see now what he said to them that were rejoicing. "Rejoice not that the spirits are subject unto you, but rather rejoice because your names are written in Heaven." Now, my friend, how on earth could their names have been written in Heaven if they were still in their sins? No thinking man can conceive of such a thing as a sinner having his name written in Heaven, while he continues in sin. We next notice in Matthew the 10th chapter and the 7th and 8th verses, "And as ye go preach saying the Kingdom of Heaven is at hand, heal the sick, cleanse the leper, raise the dead, cast out devils, freely ye have received, freely give." The reader will notice that this text will floor any man on earth who takes the ground that the disciples were never converted until Pentecost, and I notice in my Bible that this text is marked two years before Pentecost, and in a little contest with a preacher who said the disciples were never converted until the day of Pentecost, I showed him the 8th verse and said to him, "Brother, what had the disciples received freely and were to give freely?" Now, I said, "Tell me what these men had received." Well, he said they had re-

ceived money and were to go out and help the poor;
that's what they had received. Well, now I said to
him, "That would have been a blessed work, and hon-
ored of the Lord, but these men had not received money
for the 9th verse says, "Provide neither gold nor silver
nor brass nor scrip in your purse." Now, I said, "Brother, there they go to preach the Gospel without gold or
silver or brass or scrip in their purse, and yet they had
received freely and were to give freely." Now, I said
to him, "Now tell me what these men had received."
Now, he took this turn on me and said, "They had received clothing and were to go out and divide up clothing among the poor." Well, I said again, "A man could
not do a more worthy work than to give clothing to the
poor, but the 10th verse says, "Take one coat and no
shoes with you." Now, I said, "Brother, did it ever oc-
cur to you that a preacher out holding meetings with
one pair of breeches and stark barefooted, could not
give away clothing." So I say the same to you dear
reader. He backed off and came at me again and said
the disciples had received wisdom and were to go out
and give freely. Now, I said, "Brother, the Bible speaks
of two kinds of wisdom, Spiritual and worldly; which
kind had these men received?" and he said, "Spiritual
wisdom." Well, I said, "Amen, that is just what I have
been contending for, if a man has received spiritual
wisdom it is because he has been born again, for no
man has spiritual wisdom without being born again,
and then to my surprise he took this turn on me, and
said, "No, it was worldly wisdom they had received."
Well, now I said, "Old boy, hold your breath a minute

and I will knock you off the Christmas Tree." Now, I said, "Turn and read in Acts 4:13, 'And when they saw the boldness of Peter and John, and perceived that they were ignorant and unlearned men they marveled and took knowledge of them that they had been with Jesus.' " Now, I said, "Brother, there they go to preach the Gospel and they have been chosen and ordained of the Lord; and freely they had received and freely they were to give and they had no gold nor silver nor brass nor scrip, but one coat and no shoes, and no sense." Now, I said, "What in the world had they received freely?" and then at this time he said he supposed they had been converted, and that ended the contest, or the fight. I didn't win in the struggle, but thank the Lord, the old Book did. If a man stands by the old Book as the soldier stands by his gun, thank the Lord he will win every time. Glory be to God on high.

We next notice a few more verses. In the 10th chapter of Matthew's Gospel, we begin in the 11th verse and read down to the 17th, "And into whatsoever city or town ye shall enter, inquire who in it is worthy; and there abide till you go hence. And when ye come into a house, salute it, and if the house be worthy let your peace come upon it, but if it be not worthy, let your peace return to you. And whosoever shall not receive you nor hear your words, when ye depart out of that house or city, shake off the dust of your feet. For verily I say unto you, it shall be more tolerable for the land of Sodom and Gomorrah in the day of Judgment than for that city. Behold, I send you forth as sheep in the midst of wolves, be ye therefore wise as serpents and harmless as doves." Now, reader, you will bear me witness that every line in these six verses of Scripture prove to any thinking man or woman on earth that these men were converted. We will notice first that Jesus said, "Into whatsoever city or town ye shall enter, inquire who in it is worthy, and there abide till ye go thence."

Now, reader, listen to me just one minute. If these men were unregenerated sinners and yet in the gall of bitterness and in the bond of iniquity, any house in town was plenty good enough for them, and you are saying so too while you read these words.

The next step I take is this. We will notice now that Jesus said if the house be worthy, let your peace come upon it. Now, stop and think for a minute. What kind of peace is He talking about? Well, now let's read a few more words and see for ourselves. In Isaiah's prophecy, in the 57th chapter and 21st verse, He says, "There is no peace saith my God to the wicked." Then you see at a glance that these men were not sinners for God said that the sinners were without peace, and Jesus said to these men, "Let your peace come upon the house if the house be worthy." Now, if you want to know what kind of peace Jesus was talking about, turn to Rom. the 5th chapter and read the first verse, "Therefore, being justified by faith, we have peace with God, through our Lord Jesus Christ." Now, here we find out what kind of peace these disciples were in possession of. Peace with God, and that only comes when a man repents of his sins and believes on the Lord Jesus Christ, and when he does that he receives this peace from Heaven, right on the spot, this wonderful peace. Well, amen, and glory to God. How well I remember in sorrow's dark night, when the lamp of His word shed its beautiful light. More grace He has given and burdens removed, and over and over His goodness I have proved. And I say hallelujah!

We next notice the words of Jesus in conversation with these disciples. He says, "Whosoever will not receive you nor hear your words when ye depart out of that house or city, shake the dust off of your feet. Verily I say unto you it shall be more tolerable for the land of Sodom and Gomorrah in the day of Judgment than for that house or city." Now, dear reader, just one thing I want you to see. If these men were unregenerated sinners and Jesus sent them out to preach the Gospel, knowing at the time they were sinners, and said at the same time that if the people you all preach to don't receive the message that ye sinners deliver to them, it will be easier on Sodom and Gomorrah in the day of Judgment than for them. Jesus Christ would have made Himself one of the greatest monsters on earth. Why should the people receive their message if they were a crowd of sinners? A sinner sent out to preach is no better than the sinner who stays at home, and you know it. How unreasonable it looks to think of Jesus sending out twelve sinners to preach the Gospel with the understanding that if the people did not get religion under the preaching of these twelve sinners, it would be easier on Sodom than on the people who heard these disciples and failed to get converted under their ministry. What a thought! Just think it over

again and see where the man puts himself who takes
the ground that the disciples were never converted until the day of Pentecost. Don't you see that if the disciples went out preaching without any salvation that
all the sinners in the country would have had a perfect
right to have risen up and demanded that these disciples get salvation themselves before coming to them to
get them converted? Who can deny this fact?

The next thing I want you to notice is found in the
16th verse. Christ said, "I send you forth as sheep in
the midst of wolves, and be ye therefore as wise as serpents and as harmless as doves." Now, reader, you
know all through the Bible that God's people are com-
pared to sheep and in this verse Jesus Christ said that
His disciples were sheep, and the sinners that they were
to preach to were wolves. If the disciples were sinners
themselves what would have been the difference between them and the other wolves that they were to
preach to? Can you see any difference? Well, if you
take the ground that the disciples had never been converted you can't, but if you look at them in the Bible
light, you will see a set of saved men preaching to a lot
of unsaved men. And again He said, "Be as wise as
serpents." How in the world could He have used such
language if the disciples were yet unregenerated sinners, for no sinner is as wise as a serpent. The old Book
said that the sinner is a fool, and God said to him, "Thou
fool, this night thy soul shall be required of thee." And
again, "the fool hath said in his heart, There is no
God." We will notice the last clause of this verse.
"Be ye as harmless as doves." Now reader, I just

simply hang you up on this one clause, and let you kick and rare until you wear yourself out. Don't you know a sinner is not as harmless as a dove. And again if there had been any harm in a dove Jesus never would have said to a preacher, "Be ye as harmless as a dove." Whoever caught a dove doing wrong? And on the other hand, who ever caught a sinner doing anything else only harm? A dove is the most harmless thing in the world, and a sinner is the most wicked thing on earth. You see they are just as far apart as they can be. One full of good and the other full of evil. From the day that Noah put his hand out through the window of the Ark and took the dove in with the olive leaf in her mouth, and also from the day that Jesus stood on the banks of the Jordan and the Holy Ghost came down from Heaven like a dove and abode on him, men have seen something beautiful about the life and character of a dove.

We next notice the 19th and 20th verses of this 10th chapter. Christ said to them, "But when they deliver you up take no thought of how or what ye shall speak for it shall be given you in the same hour what ye shall speak for it is not ye that speaketh but the Spirit of your Father which speaketh in you." This text locates the disciples in the family of God, and not only that but puts the Spirit of God in them, and not only that but the Spirit of God in them is telling them what to say when they get into a hard place. Reader, did ever you see a sinner in the family of God, and the Spirit of God in him, telling him what to say in a case of emergency? No, of course you did not, for God's Spirit does not abide in the sinner, therefore, the sinner is not in the family of God, and that being the case, these men were not sinners.

Now, reader, you will bear in mind that there is but one way to get into the human family and that is by the gateway of the physical birth, and that is true of the Heavenly family. There is but one way to get into God's family, and that is by the Spiritual birth. Jesus Christ said to a learned doctor one night, "Art thou a Master in Israel and knowest not these things?" And the reader will remember that Jesus had just said to him, "Ye must be born again." So without any more fuss about it, we will leave these disciples right where we found them in the family of God and God's Spirit dwelling in them, telling them what to say. Bible scholars tell us that the 20th verse is the highest form of inspiration in the Book; the Spirit of God in a man telling him what to say, and yet I have heard it preached so often that the disciples were never converted until Pentecost. Well, reader, you are convinced by now that if the disciples were never converted until Pentecost, that they were not like the sinners in our day. You see a man in God's family with God's Spirit in him, is not like the sinners of the twentieth century. In our day they have everything but God, and they don't seem to want Him at all, but as these scriptures prove that these men were converted before Pentecost, we hasten on to show you a few more Scriptures while it is day, for the night cometh when no man can work, so said our blessed Master.

We next notice the 17th chapter of John's Gospel.

I think every verse in this remarkable chapter proves that the disciples were converted before Pentecost, but we have not the time nor space to discuss each verse, but will just give you a clipping from this chapter. Now notice the 9th verse. "I pray for them and pray not for the world, but for them which thou hast given me for they are thine." Here Jesus makes a distinction between the disciples and the world. Well, now reader, you know if the disciples were still sinners that there was no difference in the world between them and any other sinner, but thank the Lord Jesus said that there was a difference. The disciples were saved, the world was not.

We next look at the 14th verse. Jesus said again, "I have given them thy word, and the world hath hated them because they are not of the world, even as I am not of the world." Now, reader, open your two eyes good and wide and take one honest look at this 14th verse, and if ever you had any doubt about the disciples being converted men before Pentecost, they will all be swept away, for Jesus said that they are not of the world, even as I am not of the world. Now reader, where would you locate Jesus religiously speaking among the saved or the unsaved? Well, you say among the saved, of course. Well, just where you put Jesus, He puts the disciples, and now, folks, there is no use of us to wherefore and whereas and resolve and resolute, and turn around and around, just like a dog who lays down in the middle of the floor and turns around two or three times looking for the head of his bed, but let's be honest with our souls and with the word of God, and if we don't believe in Holiness let's just deny the Scriptures, for the Scriptures teach conversion at one time, and bless the Lord, Sanctification at another time, which makes the two works of grace.

Now, in the 17th verse, Christ said to His Father, "Sanctify them through thy truth, thy word is truth." Now, the reader will notice that these men in the 17th verse that Jesus wants His Father to sanctify are the same ones that He described in the 14th verse and said, "They are not of the world, even as I am not of the world." So without a doubt you see that Jesus wants the people sanctified who are already converted. In fact, reader, can you find a place in the Bible where Jesus ever talked about getting sinners sanctified. No, I know you can't for there is not a passage of Scripture between the lids of the Bible that teaches that a sinner can be sanctified.

Now, the next step I take is this. I have known some men to get up and preach and say, "Oh, I believe in Sanctification as strong as you all and I believe Jesus meant just what he said in the 17th verse, but I believe we get the blessing when we come to die." Well, now reader, let me help you over that pair of steps. You notice in the 15th verse that Christ said, "I pray not that thou shouldst take them out of the world, but that thou shouldst keep them from the evil one. Now, reader, here is the point I want you to see. In the 17th verse He wants them sanctified and in the 15th verse He wants them kept in the world. Now, don't you see if they are sanctified and then kept in the world they don't have to wait till they die to get sanctified? I believe every man and woman in America that will read this tract and be honest with their souls will see that the disciples were converted before Pentecost. Now, let's take one more look at them before we go on. Christ said, "They are not of the world, even as I am not of the world." He said they had been taken out of the world, and then Christ said, "I want them sanctified and kept in the world." Now, for what purpose did He want them kept in the world? That the world might know that He had sent them into the world. The Prophet Ezekiel says in the 36th chapter and 23rd verse, of his prophecies, "And the heathens shall know that I am the Lord, saith the Lord God, when I shall be sanctified in you before their eyes." I believe that Ezekiel said what he meant and meant just what he said. And I take another step. I believe he was moved by the Holy Ghost to say exactly what he did say for St. Peter said that the Holy men of old spake as they were moved by the Holy Ghost. Now, the next point I want to clear up is this. I affirmed in the opening of this discussion that the disciples were converted before Pentecost, and also that they were not backslidden when they received the Pentecostal Baptism. Now, reader, the reason I want to make the last point clear is because from many pulpits it is preached that the blessing that came to the disciples on the day of Pentecost was nothing but a restoration from a backslidden state, and if that be true, we are still without a Scriptural warrant for our doctrine, but you will please turn with me to Luke the 24th chapter and read from the 48th to the 53rd verse. "And behold, I send the promise of my Father upon you, but tarry ye in the city of Jerusalem until ye be endued with power from on high. And He led them out as far as Bethany, and He lifted up His hands, and blessed them. And it came to pass, while He blessed them, that He was parted from them, and carried up into Heaven. And they worshipped Him, and returned to Jerusalem with great joy; and were continually in the temple, praising and blessing God." Well, amen, for such an experience as they had at least ten days before Pentecost.

Now, reader, I just want you to look at a few facts with me, and we will see whether or not the disciples were backslidden at Pentecost. In the 49th verse Christ said to wait for the promise of the Father; in the 50th verse he led them out as far as Bethany and lifted up His hands and blessed them; in the 51st verse, He was parted from them and carried up into Heaven; in the 52nd verse, they worshipped Him and returned to Jerusalem with great joy; and in the 53rd verse they were continually in the temple, praising and blessing God.

Now reader, just take one more look with me and we will let you depart in peace. First, they were waiting for the promise of the Father; second, they were worshipping Jesus; third, they had great joy; fourth, they were continually in the temple, and fifth, they were praising and blessing God. Oh, for 5,000,000,000 just such backsliders as the disciples were the last ten days of their lives before they received their Pentecost.

Now, reader, as I have proven my two points as clear as the noonday sun, I want to take a few minutes

of your precious time to look at a few of the rich promises that Jesus told them to wait for. You will notice
that Jesus said in Luke 24:49, "And behold, I will send
the promise of my Father upon you." Now, don't you
see something promised to somebody, and that that
somebody had not yet received, and if you will look
right close you can see somebody waiting for that
promise. I say amen, we are just about to get to the
shouting point, for if you will listen you can hear the
rushing as of a mighty wind, and if you will look you
can see cloven tongues like as of fire. And behold, they
are sitting on preachers and not on sinners, and if you
want to hear a noise now, just listen and you will hear
all Jerusalem in an uproar. Well, what in the world
is the matter? Why, the day of Pentecost has fully
come, and they were all filled with the Holy Ghost
and began to speak as the Holy Ghost gave them utter-
ance. In order to strengthen your faith, turn to Acts 1:4,
"And being assembled together with them, commanded
them that they should not depart from Jerusalem, but
wait for the promise of the Father, which saith He, ye
have heard of me." And in Acts 2:39, "For the promise
is unto you and to your children, and to all that are afar
off, even as many as the Lord our God shall call." Even
so amen, come Lord Jesus, and come quickly and break
the grip of the devil and sin on this old world and set
up thy blessed Kingdom, and fill the earth with thy
glory, as the waters cover the sea, Amen. "Blessed be
the God and Father of our Lord Jesus Christ, which
according to His abundant mercy hath begotten us
again unto a lively hope by the resurrection of Jesus
Christ from the dead." 1st Peter 1:3.

www.ingramcontent.com/pod-product-compliance
Lightning Source LLC
Chambersburg PA
CBHW030010040426
42337CB00012BA/722